Pity the Drowned Horses

Andrés Montoya Poetry Prize

Pity the Drowned Horses

Sheryl Luna

University of Notre Dame Press   Notre Dame, Indiana

Published by the University of Notre Dame Press
Notre Dame, Indiana 46556
www.undpress.nd.edu

Manufactured in the United States of America

Library of Congress Cataloging-in-Publication Data
Luna, Sheryl, 1965–
Pity the drowned horses / Sheryl Luna.
p.   cm.
Winner of the first Andrés Montoya Poetry Prize.
ISBN 0-268-03373-0 (acid-free paper)
ISBN 0-268-03374-9 (pbk. : acid-free paper)
1. Mexican-American Border Region--Poetry.   I. Title.
PS3612.U534P58   2005
811'.6—dc22
                                    2005001220

∞ *This book was printed on acid free paper.*

for my mother Ida

Contents

Acknowledgments   ix

I

Bones   3

Organ Failure   5

Her Back, My Bridge   7

The Dance   9

Ambition   11

The Cordova Bridge   13

Slow Dancing with Frank Pérez   15

Woman as a River Between Borders   16

II

Running   21

The Child   24

Trying Too Hard to Sing Ballads Beneath Stars   26

Gravel, Stones   28

Blazing   30

Learning to Speak   32

The Falling Apart   33

River Ghost   35

III

Bayou Trolling   39

Two Girls from Juárez   41

After Sylvia Plath   42

Poesía de Maquiladora   43

Learning the Blues after Mozart   44

Two Songs   46

Dear Mentor   48

The Bullfight   50

IV

Pity the Drowned Horses   55

Sonata on Original Sin   57

Mercury in Retrograde   60

Las Alas   62

An Atheist Learns to Pray   64

The Colt   65

The Rising Silence   66

Fence on the Border   67

Elemental   69

An Agnostic Learns to Pray   71

Acknowledgments

Special thanks to the Institute for Latino Studies at the University of Notre Dame, Robert Vasquez, Orlando Menes, and Francisco Aragón for the creation and realization of the Andrés Montoya Poetry Prize and their generous support. Sincere thanks to Rachel and Alberto, Dawn and Zenon, and praise for my mother Ida and my grandmother Mary, whose faith and many sacrifices led to this book.

I would also like to thank the editors of the following publications, where many of these poems have appeared, at times in earlier versions:

The Amherst Review: "The Falling Apart"

Borderlands: Texas Poetry Review: "The Bullfight"

BorderSenses: "Woman as a River Between Borders" (as "River Between Borders")

Dánta: A Journal of Poetry: "Bayou Trolling," "Dear Mentor," and "Two Girls from Juárez"

The Georgia Review: "Bones"

The Haight Ashbury Literary Journal: "Learning to Speak"

The Hawai'i Review: "An Agnostic Learns to Pray," "After Sylvia Plath," "Trying Too Hard to Sing Ballads Beneath Stars," and "Las Alas"

Horizons: "The Colt"

Kalliope: A Journal Of Women's Art and Literature: "An Atheist Learns to Pray" (as "Faith")

The Madison Review: "Pity the Drowned Horses"

New Delta Review: "Slow Dancing with Frank Pérez"

Notre Dame Review: "Sonata on Original Sin" and "Fence on the Border"

The Pacific Review: "River Ghost"

Poetry Northwest: "The Cordova Bridge" and "Her Back, My Bridge"

Poems and Plays: "Ambition"

Prairie Schooner: "Organ Failure" and "The Dance"

Puerto del Sol: "Poesía de Maquiladora"

Spoon River Poetry Review: "Gravel, Stones"

I

Bones

Once, as a girl, she saw a woman shrink
inside herself, gray-headed and dwarf-sized,
as if her small spine collapsed. Age
and collapse were something unreal, like war
and loss. That image of an old woman sitting
in a café booth, folding in on herself, was forgotten
until her own bones thinned and hollowed,
music-less, un-fluted, empty.

She says she takes shark cartilage before she sleeps,
a tablet or two to secure flexibility and forget
that pain is living and living is pain.

And time moves like a slow rusty train
through the desert of weeds, and the low-riders
bounce like teenagers young and forgiving
in her night's dream. She was sleek in a red dress

with red pumps, the boys with slick hair, tight jeans.
She tells me about 100-pound canisters of lard
and beans, how she could dance despite her fifth
child, despite being beaten and left
in the desert for days, how she saw an angel
or saint glimmer blonde above her, how she rose
and walked into the red horizon despite
her husband's sin.

I'm thinking how the women
in my family move with a sway, with a hip
ache, and how they each have a disk
slip. The sky seems sullen, gray, and few birds
whisk. It's how the muse is lost

in an endless stream of commercials, how people
forget to speak to one another as our ending skulks
arthritically into our bones, and the dust
of a thousand years blows across the plain,
and the last few hares sprint across a bloodied
highway. Here in the desert southwest, loss
is living and it comes with chapped lips,
long bumpy bus rides and the smog of some man's
factory trap. And there are women everywhere
who have half-lost their souls
in sewing needles and vacuum-cleaner parts.
In maquiladoras there grows a slow poem,
a poem that may only live a moment sharply
in an old woman's soul, like a sudden broken hip.

And yet, each October, this old woman rises
like the blue sky, rises like the fat turkey vultures
that make death something beautiful, something
towards flight, something that circles in a group
and knows it is best not to approach death alone.

Each October she dances, the mariachis yelp
and holler her back to that strange, flexible youth,
back to smoky rancheras and cumbias, songs
rolling in the shadows along the bare Mexican hills.
She tells me, "It's in the music, where I'll always
live." And somehow, I see her jaw relax,
her eyes squint to a slow blindness
as if she can see something I can't.

And I remember that it is good to be born of dust,
born amid cardboard shanties of sweet gloom.
I remember that the bare cemetery stones
in El Paso and Juárez hold the music, and each spring
when the winds carry the dust of loss there is a howl,
a surge of something unbelievable, like death,
like the collapse of language, like the frail bones
of Mexican grandmothers singing.

Organ Failure

When my grandfather drew his last breath
he turned to my mother's pink face, her beehive
prom-hair. He whispered fire, "There's no such thing
as a friend mijita." His heart then gave out.

And life is like his heart, all fat, all grease,
pink flush, love-hate. He was raised on menudo
tripe and burned tortillas. Friends swarmed him.
Their honey need forever hurt him before the stings,
before he lost his soul in their factories.

He sold grapefruits in a wooden stand;
his daughters sold eggs along dusty streets.
And I am learning the hero's dry soul,
the way hot sand darkened the streaks of his tears.
How he'd curse the wasps. My sister stung
on the cheek, running, wailing. An image transfixed,
was it all foreshadow?

It is how a hand reached forth in full youth draws back,
how some dogs run themselves thin believing in the win.
Does age make us brittle? Is it mostly the poor
who grow cranky as unsoaped leather?

Was it beauty? Adonis' blood flowering the snow?
When my friend's liver gave out she had grown thin
and selfish as any drone! How death carries a fifth-
grade pout, and the body cramps half-glorious.

The poor buy their way to aloneness.
I can hear the organs give out in rooms
where white walls echo as seashells.
Nurses scurrying to some future jet-plane vacation.
And the body a shell of liquid, swells, sways,
forgets to know.

To turn an ear, forgive a world afraid?
Her body grows cold. To give a melody
of yellow roses, a poem, my breath, only
then would I shy to hold a thinning body.
I am, as it is, too young and arrogant
to forgive or know.

Her Back, My Bridge

She sat blush-cheeked, straight-backed & beautiful,
thin-waisted & tearless at the window when she first came.
A crumbling brick sill beneath small elbows. Brown eyes

glisten, wish to receive dresses, jewels from American GI's.
The street below smelling of dead things, outhouses. Her flowered
red-green dress, panty hose rolled over bony knees. As a girl

she could dance; she'd scrub poverty with Ajax to find peace.
She stuffed her cheeks with Mexican food—*Las tinas*, big vats
of pintos, rice. Riding the Santa Fe boxcars to pick onions

in fields. Thirteen siblings screaming, sleeping. She was broken
early by a boy. Found herself on red knees, taken in an alley.
And the tears, did they come? Her eyes forever worried

by the sun. Has she seen trees sway wind, were clouds and sky
ever blue-green? Could she kill that boy, now a man
with a cast iron pan? Chihuahita's buildings red and gray

beneath the loneliest polluted sun. She's too old
to clean now. The state's lady comes twice a week
to scrub her frail back. They won't scratch

her back *hard* enough, won't dance her age away.
She's pissed. Wrestling's her favorite thing,
Picale, Picale, she screams poking the screen

with a pencil. Her shoes once rubbed ankles
raw, yet she's sway and swing, her voice a dove's call—
Jesus, Jesus. She told me one spring of the dove's hopeful

mourning in the fields. She's breathing thin now, her veins
too thick, her bones hollow, her left eye glaucoma-
silver. A bedroom mirror covered with pictures,
my own ten-year-old American face rosy and cheered.
She tells me, "I'm ready to die." Her favorite song,
"La Puerta Negra." The Black Door.

"You've got to be strong in this life
mi jita." Here I am singing the unsung positive capability
of the desert, how weeds grow orange wildflowers.

The Dance

I learned to dance cumbias and oldies, *the locomotion*
near a fenced river where small leafless trees lick black air.
Jump-back lyrics pulsed while Ki Ki's voice mimicked
the great pretender. Español then Ingles transcendent
in strobe-lit motion right through little Lucy's hips.

Now, Ki Ki's asbestos fibrous lungs bellow.
Dancers sway blameless, hateless. They picked onions
that way, rode wooden boxcars, slept together huddled,
riding Santa Fe rails to a place where onions
and sugar cane built Ki Ki mighty. He dreamed big
and cinematic. Picking and pulling,

his mother cooked beans and tortillas on a cast iron oven
hauled to a rusty train. Eyes glisten a past, *las tinas*
of pintos and chile, how he danced with Lucy
on a rancho somewhere north of Juárez. It was not blood-
splotched palms of Mexicano beggars, it was glory
that brought the music here to a greaseless carport.

The way wild loss can make us howl. The bass thumps
a piercing pace. Ki Ki trumpets life, bellows wisdom.
He's got his wife's small hand. She's four-foot eight.
Arthritic elbows and hands curve air. Breast to cheek,
the tiniest couple swaying that way.

Memory makes the hardest labored palms honey-soft,
joints and muscles pressed smoothly tight. Bodies sliding
across a cement floor like ice skaters in the desert.
Bodies spinning to cumbias. Languages prancing
in universal hip-hop. Dancing moments back,
rows and rows once picked and shucked and sold.

Ki Ki moved from the fields to the refinery;
polluted his hair gray, rocking and rolling life away.
Their marriage Dollar-Dance, Lucy pinned in paper bills
crazy-happy to *La bamba*. People singing
ay ay ay ay Canta no llores, drunken tears!
Mariachis singing, *las mañañitas*. I forgot for a time
how weary dancers laugh anger away.

Ambition

Danny Lopez was so dark that some thought he was black.
His eyes were wide and wild.
When he ran, his short frame's stride heated the streets.
Sweat trickled down his bony face, and his throat
lumped with desire, the race, the win.

We used to sit on the hood of my parents' car,
gaze at the stars. He would win state,
dash through the flagged shoot in Austin,
get a scholarship to Auburn, escape the tumbleweeds,
the dirt floors of his pink adobe home, his father's rage.
We were runners.

Our thin bodies warmed with sweat, and the moon round
with dreams of release. We lived a mile from the border;
the Tigua Indian drums could be heard in the cool evenings.
Our rhythmic hopes pounded dusty roads, and cholos
with slicked hair, low-riders, were only a mirage.

We drove across the border, heavy voices, drunk
with dreams, tequila, and hollow fears. We ran
trans-mountain road, shadows cast cold shivers
down our backs in the hundred-degree sun.
Danny ran twenty miles, finished, arms raised
with manic exultation.

The grassy course felt different beneath his spikes,
and the gun's smoke forgotten in the rampage of runners,
his gold cross pounding his chest to triumph, his legs
heedless to pain, his guts burning.

Neither of us return to the cement underpasses,
graffiti, and dry grass, though I know
the drums still beat when we look at the stars,
and our eyes flicker with ambition.
Brown children in tattered shorts still beg for pesos,
steal pomegranates and melons.

Young men with sweaty chests and muddy pants
ask my mother for work, food,
passage to that distant win
somewhere on the other side of Texas.

Today the green trees are wet with rain,
and I am too lazy to run. The desire to run my fingers
down an abdomen tight with ambition, is shaky, starved.

It's been too long since I've crossed that border,
drunk tequila, screamed victorious
at the mountain. The stars seem small tonight,
they don't burst over the sky like they did back then.

These poems, these books don't ravish me
the way Danny could, the way the race could.
His accented English broken on the wind, and his run,
his lean darkness, drove exhaustion to consummation.

The wind seems too humid in this preferred place,
and when I hear throaty Spanish spoken in the lushness,
I long for the grimy heat,
the Rio Grande's shallow passage,
the blue desert, and the slick legs of runners
along the smoggy highway.

The Cordova Bridge

I'm not writing delicate silver birds or some Southwest
aubade. I am rough in a pebbled and stickered dead sea.
And here, crazy-sad among the flowerless places
I sweat my way through the dirge of horns and radio

blues. Smog-filled air. Sweaty dark-dirty children hang
on my car. Their paper cups hold out a coinless surrender.
El Pasoans call them scam-gangs. Bumper to bumper
as a rainbow smears the sky, window-washers beg for dimes.
The streets narrow in Juárez. Gaudy green hand-painted

school buses block signs. The poor wait. A bright scholar
described las ciudades hermanas as unmoving. Blue hills,
the river's banks deceiving us to see one-sided, blind. Juárez,
me later driving in circles, cursing the mad stops, the move-over
hurriedness. El Paso's streets are wide, people erect chain-

link fences, bars over windows. They love their small plots
of land, their jalopy cars. A poet once sang a maid's daily
dread over Cordova. I think I see her sweating away.
I once drew a breath of lush serenity, words danced
as small breaths, gilded beads. But you see, I was cursed
in this dust, crystallized among charcoal frowns and smiles.

At times, anger is an unnamed cry. Must one sing lichen,
lagoons, a glint of sky, creamy white breasts? Here, men
and women living bare dance among crumbling things. A man
without a leg has hopped that bridge for thirty years eyeing
shiny red Firebirds. What was a bird of red-fire to him?

Do we all rise phoenix-like from our tumbleweeds? Rain-
wash twirls about brown knees, rolled jeans, bare feet.
Popsicle-sellers close tiny carts, cigarette boys cover
damp cartons. And I am dry as an American can be.

Slow Dancing with Frank Pérez

I called him fish-lips; Frank was all bones,
dark. His knees sunk in at the sides.
You could mistake him for a runner.
When he kissed me, he barely opened
his mouth. The tip of his tongue peeped
into my mouth, two fish sucking rubbery
lips. Fumbling and leaping like salmon
into a glorious world, its incalculable
madness and beauty still fresh.
Our breastless, peckless hurried sway.
My arches ached from moving tip-toed.
Our oafish knees and the lyrics
hummed in meaningless pulses and tones.
I remember the floor moving,
the ceiling aflame in colors. Each pain,
each trope blooms now to real meaning.
Frank never made it to twenty. He died
in a parachute accident, a broken young
body. I still see his black curls, eyes
two pits of dark innocence. And life is like this,
hurried and awkward; the way pride swells
and need takes over, all weary desire.
The way those lost speak through an old song
that lives *duende* or heart and steam, knows
what it means to touch. Smooth songs
sting something more than sexy, each word
swells to images, implodes in icons.
Memory does this, helps us live
through all the cutting borders,
the aches of our slow return to bungling
knees and bony hips.

Woman as a River Between Borders

I. *The Chihuahua Desert*

I rose early to wash the desert grime, watch
the unearthly flight of doves, the way pigeons
were poisoned incorrectly or how an elephant
was beaten with a stick. This is the way

of beginnings, women charmed by fits of language,
the cadence of bees around garbage cans,
the laughter of grackles, hot sun baking Coca-Cola
to sidewalks. Tumbleweeds and arroyos hush

day-long trips through barrios.
I am sand. My eyes grainy, tears brown,
and what of the different tones of bees or flies,
how a sting can kill us?

I'm speaking the language of smokers,
lung-full and wary, breathing a refinery chore,
my eyes black pits. Historically

I was fruit, voluptuous and campy, some might say
exotic, cheekbones native, my hips swaying.

II. *The Rio Grande*

I grew into the silence of third person, a landscape,
a mesa. I flew hard into the silence of gray smog,
my chest burning, my throat dry with the songs
of women with sagging faces, children
strapped to their bent backs.

They have become a river metaphor, a border,
a soulless chant to believers. Maquiladora workers slain
and buried in shallow graves. My palms refuse
to fold in prayer and god giggles in my red ears.

Sand pecks my skin like a drum roll in the hot wind.
The march of children, their backpacks plastic,
the way they see color a mystery, a dance, the shapes
of clouds, an elephant, a dove, a long-lost dog. They sing
song their way past the factory-circus.

III. *The Potomac*

Years later I loved a blank-faced man in tweed
who drank espresso and ate bagels in a deli outside
Washington D.C. His pale face mirrored in the glass
at a video-store where he grumbled artless
and unfilled by the hurried ache

of cicadas. His first and last job in the world
of mundane labor. He was all red hair;
his voice bellowed.

Was it the seventh or tenth year he dubbed
my language, subtitled my screens? Windows
on the metro metalled and tunneled.

I lost the desert dance of blood, half-forgot
the closed copper mine, the way the border's earth
is lead-filled and sullen.

IV. *The Vlatva*

Awed by cathedrals in Paris, then Prague,
I was the archangel of rage with my book-bag,
a wordless hum. I began to speak with my hands,

my eyes Slavic dark, searching. I worshipped
fat swans along the thick river taking in the green
wondering why I had been blessed by such beauty.

I sensed him in a snowdrift of words historically
divine. And what was he or I in this world? I didn't see
the gold specks in his eyes, the way poetry

became his glory, full of fan-fare and the strife
of strip malls. And here, envying his pristine days,
the way the books never cover his mouth,
our hearts pumping separately to the rhythm of loss.

II

Running

I was never in New England, always hated clam chowder,
the way lobsters boiled helplessly alive.
I learned to pity bothersome insects, and lizards
regrowing severed tails were gods.

I flew to Chicago, hated thick pizza, the way the Playboy
building stood steel-like and phallic beneath the gray
sky. Fell on my ass in the Wisconsin mud, running
and running, never hitting anything but shifting ground.

Wilson Cheptoo yelling *pump your arms!*
My thin arms, thin legs. *Marry me and be my mate.*
We'll live in a hut among the yellow tall grasses of Kenya,
and we'll run, we'll always run. Cheptoo would sing,
through a white-toothy smile, his bony elbows waving.
We were both lost among the blonde girls, the rush
to a laughter we couldn't really understand.

You are the next Mary Decker. You must pump
your arms, use your arms up the hill, always.
Run, run like the devil! So I ran, and I ran.
Ran marathons, cross-country meets over grass,
that green foreign beauty.

It was like Paris, the damn grass! Like Prague
and I fell in love with swans and then a lone blue heron.
Walt Whitman there tickling my thighs in Arkansas.
I was all desert, all prickly loss, the smooth
stone, the worn hill without trees, the black
hummingbird among weeds. I ran through Houston,

Los Angeles, Austin, Colorado. Indoor wooden
slanted tracks, outdoor burning black asphalt tracks,
snow covered muddy hills, fingers frozen.
I began to dream of that barren place where Spanish
swung through the air like a fast dance. I began to love
the dry things of my past, and still I ran through books,
through men, through time like a rabid dog
learning a frothy anger.

There were crosses and prayers, children
screaming, poetry readings in smoky rooms,
a schizophrenic singing on the lawn with piss
staining the crotch of his pants.
There was a gay man with stolen buddhas
planted in his underwear. And still I ran,

ran through fields of cows, fields of corn,
fields of alfalfa, streets of wild Dobermans,
streets of crack dealers, men cursing street-corner
telephones and imagined satellites. I read and read,
misthinking words something akin to wisdom.
Ran like a woman born among the bare sands.
Ran from my mother, from my absent father.

Then I stopped, winded, palms on my thighs
and saw the sky. I stood in the small town
of my losses like a widow, like an old woman
near death. Suddenly, I sat, slept, ate.
Smoking cigarettes and sipping Guinness,
I grew fat. This is the way to truth.

And I am still lost in the non-running,
my mind like ice, my heart a swollen death
coming. Watch me hobble here in sunlight.
Yet, now I walk. And it is kind and good to walk
among the faces of the hurried. My pulse is strong,
the blood flows in its slow acceptance of skin, sinew,

and bone. Here where home is a broken border
at noon and the Rio Grande shimmers
while the ragged men run and wade and swim
as if they are running for their lives.

The Child

In the steam of spring when trees rumbled wind
I lived half-dead, my face blank as a window-
smudged night, and I found that men were cruel. Dirty
pigeons beautifully perched in eloquence on wires,
the sky opened as a book of sighs.

Men are cruel, and I am smaller.
Smaller than the dots of stars, smaller than
pebbles before their wearing away. Worn
in shadows, I find my eyes blinking
death. Only the sun can save anything,

the birds sway to Mozart.
And dead men rise everywhere, stabbed
yet rising, lifting their heads to smaller stars
in mystery and desire. Lifting tight jaws to light.
It has been too long since I've seen rainbows,

the river dance of wasps, the clapping thunder,
violent necessities. Death and Beauty
hand in hand in the shadows of trees,
and the grass tickling my ankles. Oh, Life,
the abstract angel on your shoulder, and fools,

fools, everywhere in command counting umbrellas,
harassing the wind, always losing power.
I am dancing with them all, awake in the dead night,
my eyes red and unsettled. The train horn
plowing the black. As if anything were beyond

our moments. Dancing here with my small eyes,
my small hands, fingers snapping, hips swaying.
Dancing to the dying sounds of moments
back to smallness, redone like rocks
to pebbles then dust beneath tiny stars.

Trying Too Hard to Sing Ballads
Beneath Stars

Even eternity dies sometimes. I'd plunge myself
into proverbs if they'd work. I'd sing narcissus too,
if that would dance me back to magnolias or suns
but I'm a pauper and a lament.

I hunted Orion, each star a dot, an eon. Thinking
once swelled into a chore. I fist-fought the light while birds
chirped and the sky grew dark. I drew a card
with a clown, never a king, so slowly, my wrists two

calcified clicks. Our love appeared a shot of piss
against the night. Then glory flapped in a crow's crooked
wings. All I knew was to pick myself up after the dirt,
the loss, the desire. My cheeks sagged forgetfulness
after you left in a swirl of exhaust fumes and cigarettes.

I found myself widowed before marriage. My feet two heavy
plods; unforgiving, my crystal-cure rests heavy between
my breasts. Stars danced around Jupiter. Perhaps I was
a lost shoe, a given, a made. The way sky waltzes

too large & inevitable to complain. I lost my heart,
not in diving fins, masks or wrecks;
I watched my mother's hair fall out. I lost beauty,
my cup of fate. And generally sins help us live.

Among the traffic-stupor of smoggy days,
I find myself wetter than rain; alone, my cheeks
always flushed and hot. And I still know nothing
of Tangiers. Nothing of a lover's soft mouth!

Living was like this: a row of slaves, a brook
of fire. Fortune tickled my neck and left for another.
The cricket's wings were erratic and full of pain.
To be a boy who believes in God and sings bliss!

How certainty and a smooth nose make everything
a breath of angels when falling comes only as rose
petals drifting to heaven.

Gravel, Stones

It is night and music clanks like chains.
There is a red-faced girl collecting money
for the paper. She walks every morning
to darkness and cold, fingers frozen
in the forgetting. Brown haired, cycling
through gravel streets, among dying

trees, fumigated air clutching her lungs.
And there she goes pedaling her way, humming
in hard work. And her heavy army jacket
like a small whale swimming through darkness.
Handlebars jerk. Dogs bark. Dobermans chase
booted, heavy feet. And there she goes,

dreaming of some far-off warm place and cola.
She moved to New Orleans like a steamy tune.
She stood on street corners singing in a hoarse pitch,
the lips of a black man vibrating with her song,
music in the humid air like coming rain.
A decade later dancing and smoking on Bourbon

Street, hurried steps of people insignificant
and quiet in the back of her mind.
Then came D.C., the metro a silver streak.
She stood on subway cars preaching heaven
to heathens, her army jacket large and puffed,
palms like brown leaves, shaking

in the harsh wind. Her mouth opened and closed
like the sky, her teeth yellow from the water
in the old barrio. Far from D.C. and New Orleans
a memory of old improvised song. The moon
cut clean, like her heart.
She hitchhiked home from Tennessee's green canvas.

Trees there like umbrellas, the sky a green depth.
She came to know deer and buzzards on highways.
And the music came like a swan on the still lake
of her. Cars and exhaust. Crowded Greyhounds,
children cried and sniffled with colds.
She returned to cracked dry desert,

grew hard into the sadness of cardboard
shanties, found herself counting dead pigeons along
the roadside. Felt herself like a pound of flesh
among wild dogs, sang to the round sun, felt
winter come upon her as spring. And the smog,
gravel roads, the lapped roofs like prayer books,

closed. She walked the old paper route like a god, a child.
Felt again the heavy bag sling against her rusted
bike, the corroded chain falling off onto a cracked
sidewalk. Her father yelling at her to grow up.
Her brown eyes flashed something of mother's

China dolls, East Texas bluebonnets, the dark
Atlantic, the sand-specked wind. Fingers clenched,
she breathed something of smog and found a white
stallion grazing on the dry grass in the desert's glory.
She half knew of glory, and the breath she took
was deep and knowing. There were children playing

basketball on the hardtop, cement never slowing
their brown knees, their jumping gladness.
Poverty grew on her like a vast cool winery cave
where crystal glasses held by poets clink, and men
and women in beige slacks sit with legs crossed
on metal chairs. They laugh in a valley where

the price of getting there is high. And the memory
of difference drove her home to the stark desert.
She swore off her want and skipped
along gravel stones, humming again
and again into the cool morning, the sun
rising behind her small frame.

Blazing

for Ki Ki

The sky white light before the asphalt highway
stretched itself across our desert playground.
We stole the neighbor's black Harley and spray-painted
the gray school red. Wildflowers and cacti bloomed
violet and orange across dull leaves.

I wore blue and pink bows in my tangled hair.
Easter meant chocolate and Jesus. Michael so thin
and Ki Ki lived. It was before mansions scarred
the face of the blue mountain. Huge homes
rising like marble and stone monoliths

to a new kind of life, a life all art and museum,
echo upon echo in a canyon of old Byzantium. Art
like stone endurance, yet I was dirt and sweat,
brown tan where sky stings in springtime.
The canal's speckled crawdads, Abuelita's Spanish jazzy.

Winters warmed, cousins slid sand-slopes on
hot metal garbage-can lids, legs bit by wind-pecks
of earth. The dirt collecting in our ears; eyes tear-filled,
glossy. It was before we blocked the music of night stars,
as the white noise of the sun fell upon us in sleep.
Connie smiled holding her rainbow-plastic-wrapped basket.
Ki Ki in his first gray suit and black shiny shoes
lectured us all about something grave and mysterious
in the universe. Truth was vanilla ice cream

on a hot Chihuahuan desert day, a dilapidated ice-
cream truck with the sign in red: Caution Childrens!
The music full of static, and us streaming behind it
waving and waving it down. The driver
broken-toothed and dark like Christ.

Yesterday, Ki Ki's last breath burned, his mother wailing.
Life sucked something like marrow from us. Sand
in the barren place, broken pebbles, the bareness
of our desert births howled. Día de los Muertos, candles,

flames like Old Halloween nights. Us with our bags
full of all we thought sweet. I remember his fat face,
crooked smile, whispers, how we boogied
to rock-n-roll all strobe-lit and sweaty in 1979;
we fought over forty-fives and LP's spent now

like electric youth. Ki Ki Jr. died at thirty-three.
Christmas was hollow; El Paso's stars dull,
the moon shadowed with Moses' death-fog.
Ki Ki Senior's white scars became beautiful,
the left side of his body once aflame with copper

smelting. His heart later invaded by something black.
The choking smoke of his days, a factory furnace hissing
like the canyon. Without Ki Ki, without the electric
steel music of the past in our ears,
the red moon grew hot, the sky gray ash.

A red cauldron-moon blazed everything above the highway,
larger than ever, everything burning like a sun.

Learning to Speak

I forgot how to speak. The old man with a gray
beard eyed me, waiting for Spanish.

Years of English rumbled something absent, forgotten.
The Tigua Indian Village, men at the corner bench eating

tamales. Indoors, tables with white formica,
floor-tiles peeling. In the steam of cilantro and tomato

children sit cross-legged and sip caldo de res.
Men smoke afterward in faded jeans, and T-shirts lightly rise

around their pecs in the wind. It is how home is all
that's left in the end. The way we all return forever exiled.

History in mud houses and shady river-trees. Canal water
drifts. Children poke crawdads with dry branches. I spoke

Spanish broken, tongue-heavy. I was once too proud
to speak Spanish in the barrio. He waits for my voice.

His eyes generations. My brown skin a scandal on the hard streets
of El Paso. But, everyone loves a resurrection. Mauricio on a red

motor bike; Bob, a green-eyed white war hero, spits tobacco.
The sunlit desert and its gold light falling upon us. *Quiero*

aprender español, I whisper. He smiles. Blue hills
in the distance sharpen in an old elegance; the wind
hushes itself after howling the silences.

The Falling Apart

Aslam, pressing his unwanted body against mine.
Aslam, singing of graveyards and peace,
asking me to marry him when I piled into my car
to drive to another place. He said, "My home
is the grave. This is a temporary house."

We share an affection for graveyards, stones,
speak about dirt calling life to rest. My mother grows old
in poverty. I think of Jesus at times. My soul grows
arthritic and sad for answers. Aslam and flowers left behind.
I was called to the desert, to an immense absence of green,

where language is shadow and sunlight between leaves.
Neither English nor Spanish; something of both. Yucca
and lizards, dirty beggars, the ineffable beauty of rage.
Time to sing poised in perfect coughless breaths fades.
I was taught order in rainfall, and this was a lie.

Teachers pointed sticks, claimed the sky reason.
Lazily, I borrow time and taste cool rain.
Aslam, owning hotels in Bombay. My mother dying
for minimum wage. Time to sing forgetfully shameless
wanes. Factory owners live off the swollen finger joints

of women. Aslam cooking blow-fish, working twelve hours
a day, drinking scotch like water. Time to sing Sackcloth
and Ash, perfectly juxtaposed as winter then spring
fades. I was taught to claim order in green, to count rainbows,
forget all things dust-covered and brown.

All the crumbling places, pink stucco homes, unpainted faces
too grimy to sing. Aslam, shrugging off, "a poor country,
a rich one, what can we give?" Time to see the burrowed
eyes of friendless men fades. Time to dissect sunsets
into syllables dissipates.

A rich man, a ragged man, and what pennied words
could one give? I was weathered by dry days,
pondered the ineloquence of lush blowsy blues,
and I learned to cry breathless rage into silent pillows.
Time to speak such frayed things leaves.

River Ghost

Little Chihuahita shadowed beside Segundo barrio.
A dead German shepherd with a broken neck lies
on the side of the street for days. The stench
of El Paso's sewage in the air, a Mexican flag hugely
flaps itself above the chain-linked fence

topped with razor wire. In the morning blue mountains
smog. South side of the border a man jogs.
The river's bank green, small trees bob in the wind
like truffle-treats, mirage. Each day thousands cross
the open bridge, both ways,

each night they go home to sleep silence. Cars hum
and wait for hours like sleeping cats. A cemented river
half-dried, even the canal drains away. Some say droves
of shadows at night move ghost-like through the dying river.
These people grow invisible, as if air, irrelevant and holy;

at night I can hear the whisper of my grandfather,
"all the angels live in Juárez."
There is an old language broken in my throat.
Some eyes mistake me for shadow. When I speak my voice
a fearful phantom. In spring dust storms come, the sky

browns, my visage half-forms beneath the Italian cypress;
and when the day's moon is full in its silence,
I am afraid of my own darkness.

III

Bayou Trolling

Old Roy almost yodeling cuddles a bottle of brandy,
tells me of Venezuela, his unforeseen mob-marriage,
how the gun at his temple was hard and cold.
He later said, "When we get old we get ugly."

How could I tell Roy, mob-named Blackie-Diablo,
he was still a pretty devil in white wading boots,
his hair a cloud, a shirt untucked & perfectly dirty.
Treading the Gulf's gray swells, my pain lazy beneath

a cypress tree half-buried in water, two rainbows heaven
my sun-burned face. Broken shells whiten the beach
behind the factory. Roy laughed among alligators
glorying me to believe again.

His wife burned by a pan of hot grease at age six,
her left eye now blind. She birthed a handsome boy. At dawn
he trawls for shrimp among the frogs' memory-less dirge.
Did she or Roy know I lost a bit of my hurt that day?

The mucky Delta's green schemeless canals, elephant ears
wildly untouched by worried eyes. All the while, we learn
we all unknowingly lie. I had been capsized and unable
to breathe, my feet cut along hidden oyster shells. He said,

"You're a tough woman." I should've kissed him after I jumped
off his boat and later returned to New Orleans, where a silver-painted
mime strewn in Mardi Gras beads stood, a statue, winking.
"I see you," the white-faced jester sang.

Sax & cornet players sweltered on unclean streets, a jazz
singer's lips vibrated still air. Roy's son, a muscled boy,
trawls for shrimp with his father's white boots and bent
body and mislearns to blame all blacks in 1999.

Boys tap-danced for pennies. We are all of such shine,
brandy in the open throat or the moving white-eyes of a mime
performing. Our word-wounds heal, burn, as fresh water
meets the salt and magnolias weep light.

Two Girls from Juárez

Two girls from Juárez hesitantly step toward my desk.
"Ms.," one says with a paperback of Plath's *Ariel*,

corners folded and coffee stained. "Was she white
or black?" One with over-dyed red hair and black

roots announces, "She was prejudiced!"
I am now questioning my life in a desert; questioning

as lightning rips the sky like an instant of daylight
in the hard black lake of night. In Plath's "Daddy"

a black man bites a woman's heart, and all the wit
and the wordplay between darkness and light shrugs.

I am bitten. The girls want to know
about Plath's gasps, about her white

eyes in darkness. One wears an electronic
bracelet around her ankle.

The other's cheeks red with too much rouge.
I imagine they live nights dangerously

in an Oldsmobile near the Rio Grande,
that they love for real and they love to love.

I smile at them with no answer. I lost answers
long ago and the faces of my colleagues grew ghost-like

and words fell away and the poetry cancer came
like a priest for the sacrifice.

After Sylvia Plath

I changed my name back to *moon*, back to my grandparents'
name and Zacatecas. It's all river-sludge under the International
Bridge. All our fighting words hang on arthritic hips

like swords, too fragile to do anything but cut through
to the hollow bone of loss. All our words dance themselves out
of our caves, yet the blue flames at our backs warm us.

Quiet and frazzled on the wet asphalt, lightning cracks
the sky. I am seeking a lover, or the shadow of a lover, oblivion
in the chlorinated depths of a pool where my lips will remain

half-open, taking in the blueness and quiet. Tonight, the dark sky
splits open. God's voice bombs us with frightening certainty.
There's a reason we can't see god, a reason he burned

in a bush for Moses. It's an unpleasant affair,
to be burning and old, to feel your heart aflame.
Here I am longing for the blue water's silence. I'm sensing

Plath floating in words, alone, quietly drifting beyond blackness
into her blue weightless dusk, after the bombing, after being struck
and consumed by something larger than fear.

Poesía de Maquiladora

I am swept into a sadness, still
and unspeakable in sterile rooms where
men might as well wear white coats
and drink my breath from stethoscopes.

They were so happy to show us
the habits of locusts, drain blood
into plastic bags of their manufacturing.
Tell us, Latina, was it what they
assumed it was, broken language,
poetry of a lesser nature, a wound?

The way my brown knees
slammed hard in the fall
from what was left of grace.

My eyes shrunk to slits, my only
salvation came in the flight of grackles,
the way the moon swelled, striped
with red-orange light.

It has rained more this spring.
I am sick of having to watch what I say.
The grackles have beaten the songs down
with their desperate caws.
The tree branches scream too, now.

The most intelligent doctors walk
through their patients. Assume a sickness.
My mind has pleated itself
in a veil of shadows.
My body is fading
back to an invisible border.

Learning the Blues after Mozart

I.

Ling said, "Mozart is not so good
due to an absence of pain."
I never much liked the blues,

bare land expanded for miles
in an emptiness with gray skyline.
Never knew the pang, the chrome

slide, the deep open-throated bass among
the voices of women like sparrows
was in my bones, always, some milky marrow.

The thin sway of dark bodies, sweat
of loss a hurried cadence of rage.
It's when women dance hard, gyrate.

II.

Mozart frenetic like fall's first golden
waltzing; leaves flock skies. Ling like a moon
still above the Rio Grande's slow gurgle.

Watching slow ways we come to living:
moon, sky, breath, light piano touch,
the skeleton face-bone prophecy of our death,

moments delicate, flutes, harp songs.
We are the painted domes of history echoing,
whispering something of scotch and clinking glass,
dim light, a largeness in the flight of cranes,
the sky and the bloody earth.

Song can come like flame
or flower. I am often stone.
From the howl I never heard,
I rose a yellow-eyed grackle and black
among springtime, I first translated

the blues juxtaposed to a quiet sonata
of feathers falling.

III.

Ling, telling me something of pain in her songs,
mouthing it in a whiteness, an Asian quiet pluck,
hurried then slow like strings pulled tight

to create a long song, pulled tight
in a wind-filled night. The blues come survived
like scar, and people speak of rhythm

and blue. Mozart delicate, wind chimes,
a whisper, a breeze in the starlit night.
The blues electronic and wild, unrestrained,

tight and high, deep and low,
as if something young was ripped
from life. Among the plays, the stages,

the masks, I heard Ling like humility
before my wake, felt my palms forget
air, felt how the moon, in an effort to sink

deep into its painless excursion across
the vast emptiness of want,
grows into absence.

Two Songs

"Let go," you sang; my arms two long stilts of sorrow.
Even the sparrow's hunger is held in the palms of gods.
She is fed by crumb. The asphalt summer appears a pond.
I have forgotten sky in a weary need to win a title, and you,

brown-haired and light, graying gently in the lush
New England shade; are you hounded by black flies buzzing
heavy in humid sunset? Is your face still all boyish grace?
You said Texas trees were small and insignificant.

Large yellow leaves in autumn shed to the ground. Grackles
screeched my displacement. You said they were dirty.
I loved them for cawing, for shitting on old scholars.
You prostrate beneath the campus oaks reading Yeats, me

washing dishes, learning an old rage. "Anger goes nowhere,"
you said. I returned to the shock of graffiti in the barrio.
A dull mural of Mary outlined in black spray paint against
a white stucco home hums the music of exile. In these stark

borderlands where black birds fly in time with cars, I
count fire ants along the sidewalk. They work endlessly
with the burden of crumbs, walk at angles, as if gravity
were irrelevant. Hornets buzz about. I imagine you counting

beats with soft palms; words spilling out in careful recitation,
like a young boy learning a dead language. I prefer dry song,
the way the river thins and children scream in Spanish,
"esperame, esperame," but the world refuses them.

It rushes on the same axis; *nothing can be turned back.*
Children build rafts with spare twigs, the sky opens up and blows
sands in a brown heaviness. The music about the red hornets'
dance. When the rain finally comes it is as mud
driving the blue sky down.

Dear Mentor

San Francisco led me to a larger, less narrow
aesthetic. You title poems in Latin or some secret,
and there is a strange beauty in your smooth
transparencies. You led me away from clarity
into the abstract realm of loss;

the back of your neck frizzled
in its red hair. Belief in beauty
can be harsh. Your father was a doctor,
and he remains unhealed in his rage.

There is a cloying when one has too much money.
There is a sky lit in easy forgetfulness.

A landscape within a landscape.
This painting, endless like fog
rolling through the marina. Clouds above the cracked
Nevada desert. I watched them rove above tributaries
of black water, then roll into feathered fan-like wings.

My own eye white. Today, in the Palace
of Fine Arts, stone pillars touch the sky
and openness moves like the wind off the bay.
This cornea of volcanic ash. My hair a gray storm cloud.

I've become swan with my own gray neck
resting twisted on my back.
The fog rolls over the bridge like want.

A pelican with one leg, one fin-like webbed foot torn
from its body, the leg now healed, rubbery.

It's like this: talk and talk, smooth pages of a book
settled in your lap. There retiring, not on a hammock,
but rather the gold carpet of your living room.

In the longness of self, I've become cloud,
water blue then gray then white.
This is the way of things, green iris
centered in blackness.

Like starfish limbs, all healed-over,
regrowth, our scars mend like memories.
Among the pillars of stone women
who turn their round backs against us,
the sky rolls through the city.
I am a seam of light.

The Bullfight

Beer bottles hang in bare brown tumbleweeds,
rock-cement fences crumble and maquiladora
workers buried in shallow graves along the border;

Indian mothers smudged with asphalt beg for dimes
near the Tigua reservation where drums rumble
to a statue of a Spaniard long dead and the voices

of rage, and history cannot be redone like a poem.
It's something we carry, something we can never carry.
I am so far gone from the memory of myself, even Chicanas

ask me who I am. *What is your name* they say.
What is in a name? Names are like languages; they come,
they go. I am counting seashells from a trip to the bayou.

My thigh cut on an oyster shell there, green trees sang
with crickets all night as this flesh bled and bled into water.
Salty sea meets freshwater marshes, and animals slither

through grass. Alligators thin in their numbers,
hidden within themselves. Creole women singing.
The Rio Bravo slow with a muddy past. The river

that divides me, crosses me daily like the forgotten
history of my grandmother. The way her abuelita snuck
pennies beneath her pillowcase. "She was the only one

who cared," she sighs. The way children fight
among themselves. How an egg is divided
among eight crying mouths.

My legs went limp in the cold Mississippi. Lifting
my chin up to the boat again and again, I sank.
I was all desert, brown sand, cacti blooming

small red flowers. Want grew through my veins
like weeds. The Spanish I half-knew fell from lips
as water onto sand. Even the people I longed for,

la raza, forgot my face. The same one I tried to forget
always reflected in endless mirrors, the doughy hosts
of an endless penitence for the shame at my border birth.

Never Mestiza enough, never English enough.
A face always following me, demanding homage
for its vast desert. I left the barren place where men flee

shanties and maquilas and the darting murky traffic.
Ran from my stepfather's fear of my mother's language,
from my mother's half-Jewish history. Her own lost

heritage buried in a desert cemetery plot. I ran hard,
fast, for so long, that when I returned, I was exiled,
yet forever needing the place.

Perhaps I'm fighting an imaginary bull; its single eye
blinking against the sun as it slowly dies
and its dark blood seeps into the desert sand.

My blood, of necessity, will eventually seep
into the desert; it is the way of my people;
it is the way of all people: crossing borders,

learning of caliche and wind, building monuments
from mud, finding something of themselves,
losing something of themselves.

IV

Pity the Drowned Horses

It is one of those nights when you fall back into childhood
like the breeze gentle against your half-quiet ears.

The tall Italian cypress still giant to your small eyes,
the moon lopsided—still, holy, mysterious.

The clothesline droops now and the height of the line,
once a Herculean reach, is only an arm's length away.

Your feet easily plant themselves on the ground and no longer
gleefully dangle while arms stretch sinewy & young.

The stars hum still & blessed. You carry the cracked hose
to water the drying tree, & the dead grass sings a silent hymn,

the water's dribble makes you want to cry, not because the pipes
are dry like your grandmother's bones, but because the sky

is still, yet moves like the night you turned seven. Here,
the dry garden hose brings tears to your eyes, and you weep

your insignificance. The dead neighbor's white Chevy truck,
parked in the same spot for years, is gargantuan, yet invisible.

Mr. Tellez, try to remember his round face, his broad back
in a white T-shirt watering the pink and white oleanders.

Were they imagined? Was his face so unimportant? The truck
looms undisturbed and heavy. The highway buzzes where desert

once sat calmly. Cars replaced screaming children, bicycles
and the divine ritual of running through the sands native,

dark thighs sweating in what seemed an eternal sun.
And what do we care for the smallness of another? It's our

own shame, the way palms clench or eyes dart fearfully,
the way we learn gossip in shadow, talk ourselves

into believing god is listening because we are afraid,
the shadow on your pale cheek is darkened like the blue

lake of night. All you can do is eye the slow gilded stars,
the black lake of sky, memory above the forty-foot trees

through a broken branch. The moon waltzes with the veil
of night clouds and finally water gushes and the tree's roots drink

the last waters, the first waters, holy waters brought down from sky,
and you still may think of Moses and mist like you did when you

were twelve, and may still imagine god's waters crashing down
on the heads of your enemies, yet pity the drowned horses.

Sonata on Original Sin

It was all gone: memory, time, trees.
The sea an imagined. Music
a fog, and although unwhole,
I'm quiet night. No red cauldron,
no lightening eye, no quick Jesus:

Dance of mosquitoes, whirr of crickets,
a moon's fated face. The order of nature
streaks sky, and rain falls as music, smoke
rises. Work, rest in the stab

of love. Hold yourself like a warm blanket.
The saving always slow. Your Guarded song
a space of self. Love gone in the work.
Gone in a blue pin-striped suit, the appearance
of slick shoes, in the way we mouth nothing
to one another. Guarded back.
Watch it. Watch it.

Stiff chin. False hair color.
Paint your eyes my grandmother says.
Buy a girdle.

Are death and beauty bought?
Speechless and slanted in the walk,
I jog now, felt joints loosen
to the tune of suns.

Death and beauty bought in faces,
in handshakes, in flatteries and hurried steps
to buses in slick towns, where women
wear lip gloss and highlit hair, the electric
pang of music running through veins.

You played trombone like a wounded animal.
I am remembering snow on your hair in the yard,
trees capped with it. And then you came
like a ceramic doll, smiling, a music box, set
to play the same tune for years, until that break,
that Fall.

Original sin fell from our soft lips. Now,
I am cracked in red lipstick.
The old maid counting stars and loving stars.
Alone. Carpe diem! Old lantern, black and costly,
antique Chevy. The rust of poverty like lost love,
empty fiberglass pools.

My face a butterfly rash. Lupus, then a lover lost.
Then there came the ash. Oboe Slowness.
The way you walked your dog each night
over the ridge. Arroyo empty. Gutted.
Chain-linked razor wire fences always mended
and tended. The weeds overgrown. The ache,
muscle sore to the bone. This is the way of borders:

A slow series of breaths rising, falling. The way
things thirst. Tree without green, bare window
with no curtain, dog left to die.
We have to know how to play, pour like water,
patter as rain.
Beethoven was deaf.

Be Light in silence, light in noise.
I hold my rosy cheeks, my butterfly shape.
Time is breath smoked away. We were young
and flowered. We were silent
in a perfect trance of sleep,

Endless husky-throated voices of rage
turned to snow one night. Voices of women
nearby rose lighthearted with the sparrows.
I mourn the way we were afraid to kiss
beneath the oaks, the moon laughing,

the moon crying. Us at the center of the small universe.
We two stars lingered in the bodied voice of time,
rising from dirges and requiems
like dancing stars, on the chaos of a blood-sonata.

Mercury in Retrograde

The day ended badly with a broken ankle,
a jinxed printer, and a dead car. The dry yellow grass
against the sunset saved me. Roosters

pranced across a lawn of shit, proudly plumed
in black feathers, bobbing before the gray goats.
It was the first day I saw god in the quiet,

and found a mustard seed was *very* small.
There I had been for years cursing "why?"
and all the gold in the sun fell upon me.

There was a white mare in the midst
of brown smog, majestic in the refinery
clouds. Even the radio wouldn't work!

My mother limps and her hair falls out.
The faithful drive white Chevy trucks
or yellow Camrys, and I'm here golden

on the smoking shock-less bus.
I lost language in this want, each poem
dust, Spanish fluttered

as music across the desert, even weeds
tumbled unloved. The police sirens seared
the coming night, dogs howled helplessly
sad.

Lo I walk the valley of death, love
lingers in my hard eyes. Mañana never
comes just right. I mend myself in the folds

of paper songs, ring my paper bells
for empty success. *Quiero Nada,*
if I sing long enough, I'll grow dreamlike
and find a flock of pigeons, white under
wings lifting awkward bodies like doves
across the silky blue-white sky.

Las Alas

(The Wings: A mission in a downtown barrio)

The priest raises his palms to God,
a girl walks the mass with a dove
cooing between her light palms.

Women with dyed black hair clap
and sing, robust voices rise.
Children sit sleepily and Spanish

settles in the air. A guitarist sings;
the mass moves: stands, sits, kneels,
chants, "santos, santos." Necks bent

as shadowed faces gaze the tile floor.
The lady in the row of plastic chairs
in front of my row has fat ankles,

varicose veins. Displaced like a lilac
on the dry sand, I remember polyester
days, when K-mart sandals covered

the dry heels of women and church
laughter. Can one return to a desolate
past, before one *knew* one was poor,

before the luxurious perfume?
Jesus' eyes real and piercing, a doughy
host, God in my sour mouth.

What of all this faith among the oppressed?
Poor men hold themselves straight
when their backs cramp. The priest at Las Alas

mission wears a white robe
unlike priests in large stained-glass parishes.
Other priests wear silky robes with gilded

ribbons. His robe is sheet-like, sparse,
and his Spanish twangs of Arkansas.
Men in polyester slacks and dirty jeans

stand shameless; calloused hands with imagined
doves, sea of dark bodies, steady lapping
of palms giving up and letting go.

An Atheist Learns to Pray

Maybe you found the moon sun-lit in black
space or gazed at Saturn's blue-red-gold prism.
Slow warmth in an empty universe, light
became your daily bread, night a starry
sacrifice. The way darkness paints and blots
havoc. We always return to beauty
after the abyss, bruised and cold, learning
that a rose open to May is unburdened.
Why not swing our hips, and sway as leaves chime
to dawn. One learns from children, a dog's thick
ribbed breath, the rise and fall of night. Even
when slandered one drinks water and the sky.
Blessed be the way caught among showers,
the sun later rising like a man listening to God.

The Colt

The sky glowed its red burning, and the damp
    air smelled of mulch, and the earth called
itself up inside of me like a smoggy song.
    The colt's belly round like a donkey's,
wet and frizzled brown hair trotting

behind a brown-white spotted mare,
    proud in its tall-legged towering.
Thin-ribbed dogs running through traffic.
    We call far into the distances between us.
Wind brushes my cheek in a cold need.

All things, drawn to one
    another like the flippant tail of a colt
in a barren field where the flat bed
    of an eighteen-wheeler rusts and the tractor
rests upon its fat tires, and the black eyes

of birds, the wings of crows flutter
    with a deep-throated call of hunger, want
like a cool shadow over the broken
    neighborhood. Chickens like the fretted
hard strums of electric guitars run wired

through the yard, squawking then beating the sky.
    And there stood a child like an old god,
running, nipping at the larger horses' legs,
    wild with the birthing, fresh before the earth,
the wind nothing but its very breath.

The Rising Silence

I am tired and painted and silent among boys
and teachers who think words are more than sky.

There's a mourning dove in the drying grass
and a man spouts cultural theory and ignores me.

I am worn, like the frayed wings
of a brown hawk; cold as a shadow on the moon's

cratered face, then in the dark beauty of God's
grace, I rose like Egypt, like Prussia, then Rome.

My shadow stretched across nations, singing
the last flicker of want. Shameless men

and women with tearless faces, children with swollen
knees, and I saw the ghost of man fly through black

space; fearless and hollow he sang so sadly,
yet again he looked through me.

I am air and blue sky, oblivion in the depths
of a clear pool. Like a ghost, like a shapeshifter,

I fly with my dark shadow, my wounded wings,
fly to save my last broken claw, fly away to save

my frayed feathers, my golden eye. There's a blue
rising along the desert mountainside where small

cacti fan sky. An old hawk swerves and rises
above brambles and thorns; brown-winged
and savage she lifts the sky.

Fence on the Border

It is in the bending and the pain,
the way old paint scrapes off old wood,
the way elders light our way through time
on their way to a smaller frailty.

A halo about the painted head of Jesus
on the yellow wall of *Our Lady of the Valley*
Church fades where teachers make a pittance,
richly among brown-faced children.

A burlap robe on a dark pilgrim walking
up Mount Cristo Rey with sandals as sunset
blurs a perfect pink, like the palm of God pressing
down on the bent heads of the broken,

who learn prayer amidst a harshness
I have yet to know. The barrio full of narrow
streets, adobe homes, and sweet yucca flowers
bud in the air like a rainy night.

There's a way the sand clings to the wind
and the sands brown the sky in a sadness
that sings some kind of endless echo of the border,
where the chain-link fence stretches for miles

and miles and the torn shirts of men flap
from the steel like trapped birds.
The river is narrow and appears slow.
The cardboard shanties of Colonias unveiled

among the vast open desert like ants.
The faces of the poor smiling and singing
as if sunset were a gift; the desert blooms
red and white flowers on the thinnest sparest cacti,

groundhogs breathe coolly in the earth.
And here, on Cinco de Mayo the cornea of god
glints faintly in a thin rainbow;
the hands of god rest over the blue hills,
the song of god in the throats of sparrows.

Bless You.
Bless You.

This is the way the border transfigures greed,
shapes it into something holy,

and paisanos stand alert; even pigeons soar
with something akin to the music of the spheres,
and Spanish flutters through the smoke
that burns through our small lives.

Elemental

An operatic crescendo, a soft ballad clinging
to hope, a wild sandstorm in the stinging sand.

A race to nowhere with the heavens falling,
oceans churning themselves, darkness clouding

the few distant stars. When the lighthearted verses
of happy women burn halleluiahs; what can one do
but ride the wave or be drowned? Eyes

of men vacant in their masks, this veil of loss
clouds glances. It's when we are left smiling
to no one, least of all ourselves.

when our wrists ache, when we believe
God died on a tree beneath the thunder,
when there is nothing to believe, but our own

flogging, our own dreams beneath blankets,
asleep, our eyes covered by immediate warmth.
Our mouths speaking the nothingness within.

Who could not but sing for the gilded moon,
the thin drifting sky of ourselves, mountains
but dark shadows in the night, stars passing over

our squandered moments, small storms
passing through us in our rushed blood,
thinning, slowing. The music of fear

trumpets, fades into silence. Impulsive
and afraid of our shadows, eyes like small suns,
mouths like black holes, ears like tunnels

that never meet. Feet like stone,
legs like fire, shins winged in the thin air.
We learn to sing through the fire, a hot summer

in the desert of our lives,
like pink hibiscus bloomed and trimmed;
the earth beneath us. The river as a border

is what's left of Colorado's snow and the dreams
of all of us rushing, streaming to a final slow
alluvial, silty amidst sandstorms. *Las arenas*
blowing our wild hair, our wild need, all sweat, all shiver.

An Agnostic Learns to Pray

I am history-less and the Rio Grande is nothing but a border
of dust-blown spring when the throats of mariachis open
a deep husky song like hawks, like the haunted souls
of dust-blown centuries.

There's a beaten guitar and the dry palm of its player
is beating the wood in time and the Spanish is only half
decipherable like the howl of the wind.

Memory is like the sand—grainy, harsh,
dry.

There's a lady with polyester green pants crying
because she can't learn math or pay the mortgage on her lost life.
It sits decaying in the wind,
a plastic bag covers the hole among the broken bricks
of her home, and the large clay plot of land,
that had her fooled into believing that life was an orchestra,
dries.

The land is barren and dark like the caliche-deep eyes
of a mariachi player who is angry that the men
in pressed suits will not place ten dollars in his hand
for a song. Song is like that, throaty like a mourning dove
singing on the desolate sand.

It is full of something akin to falling, and finding
the wounds in one's side healing like resurrections or births,
always rising in white scars like the birds flying
into the blinding sun.

Even the moon offers its solace like a lover
that will never leave. Sometimes we find its arrival
in the guitar strum or the trombone moan.
Art brings all things possible to the feet of the poor.

I've never washed a man's feet out of some selflessness
within, so it's difficult to know
what it means or why it's necessary to wash the feet
of some man whose face is above my own like the moon,
whose voice becomes godlike and surreal.
And I swore only when the earth was bountiful,
and justice found my door, I would begin to kneel
as if before the maker of this endless starry universe,
as a thankful fool. Now, my forehead finds the floor
and the church bells ring after decades among the artless.

I heard god among the stars and felt his kiss in the breeze,
and though I doubted his face and his feet, I began to wash,
if only for a moment, the sadness from my want.

And the sky sang and the birds hopped along the sand
as if the world were young and the music came forth
like the parting of the red sea, like the burning of bush,
like tea-leaves falling and darkening the sea;
and the shadow of a ragged hawk fell across my face
as I walked along the driest mountain in the nation,
and there were no camels,
and there were men carrying cardboard signs, begging
for something other than a song.

I envy the woman who learns prayer when her throat is dry,
lives something like faith and forgiveness
when the sky is a blizzard of brown
or the dust has blown her skin wrinkled and terse.
I envy how she sings before a statue of blank-eyed Mary,
how she lights a candle and blazes with its flame.

About the Author

SHERYL LUNA was born in El Paso, Texas. She holds a doctorate in Contemporary American Literature from the University of North Texas and master's degrees from Texas Woman's University and the University of Texas at El Paso. She has been a finalist for the National Poetry Series book awards, as well as the Perugia Press Intro Award for women poets. Her work has appeared in various literary journals, including *Georgia Review, Prairie Schooner, Borderlands: Texas Poetry Review, Poetry Northwest,* and *Amherst Review,* among many others. She currently teaches at the Metropolitan State College of Denver in Denver, Colorado.